COLLINS AURA GARDEN HANDBOOKS

HERBACEOUS PERENNIALS

DAVID JOYCE

COLLINS

Products mentioned in this book

Benlate + 'Activex' 2	contains	benomyl
ICI Mini Blue Slug Pellets	contains	metaldehyde
'Nimrod'-T	contains	bupirimate/pirimicarb
'Rapid'	contains	pirimicarb
'Sybol'	contains	pirimiphos-methyl

Products marked thus 'Sybol' are trade marks of Imperial Chemical Industries plc
'Benlate' is a registered trade mark of Du Pont's
Read the label before you buy: use pesticides safely

Editors Maggie Daykin, Joey Chapter
Designer Chris Walker
Production Controller Craig Chubb
Picture research Moira McIlroy

First published 1990 by
William Collins Sons & Co Ltd
London · Glasgow · Sydney
Auckland · Toronto · Johannesburg

© Marshall Cavendish Limited 1990

British Library Cataloguing in Publication Data

Joyce, David
  Herbaceous Perennials. — (Collins Aura garden handbooks).
  1. Herbaceous perennials
  2. Title
A CIP catalogue record for this book is available from the British Library

ISBN 0-00-412526-6

Typeset by Litho Link Ltd., Welshpool, Powys, Wales
Printed and bound in Hong Kong by Dai Nippon Printing
Company

Front cover: Lupins by Michael Warren
Back cover: Monarda didyma by The Harry Smith Horticultural
Photographic Collection

CONTENTS

INTRODUCTION

The main reason many herbaceous perennials are grown is for their quality as flowering plants; a great number are superb, either in the garden or for cutting. But no less valuable is the often exceptionally beautiful foliage. Also, the choice is so vast that good perennials can be found for almost every situation and to provide a long succession of flowering periods. All of this, combined with their ability to get on with other plants such as shrubs and bulbs makes them particularly valuable in the modern garden.

A brief history Herbaceous perennials have long been cultivated in European gardens, although not always in the first instance as ornamentals. Many began their garden careers as culinary herbs or on account of supposed or real medicinal properties. For example, one of the loveliest cottage-garden favourites, the apothecaries' paeony *(Paeonia officinalis)*, has a reputation as a healing herb that goes back to classical times. The herbals of the sixteenth and seventeenth centuries record the almost forgotten medicinal credentials of many well-known perennials but show, too, an appreciation of other qualities that make us still glad to grow these plants in our gardens.

The core of steadfast perennials that have been grown for at least the last 400 or 500 years are mainly European in origin. To these have been added, especially in the last two centuries, a vast number of introductions from all over the temperate world. Many of the finest were found in the wild. But garden-making in the East goes back many centuries, no other country in the world having a longer continuous tradition than China. European collectors found in the plant-rich countries of China and Japan magnificient perennials that had been bred and selected for centuries, among them the Chinese paeonies from which so many modern hybrids have been derived.

The cottage-garden medley of perennials and other plants, useful and ornamental, has a long unbroken history, but in other gardens the manner of growing plants has reflected changing fashions. In

RIGHT Traditional style long border with the taller flowering plants ranged along its centre and flanked back and front by plants of graduated height. A lovely and inspiring sight.

BELOW LEFT Soft 'blue' tones of stately, blue agapanthus, grey-green artemisia, and pink sedums and asters, perfectly complementing one another in both form and colour.

grand gardens there have been periods, particularly in the second half of the nineteenth century, when perennials have been somewhat neglected in favour of growing bedding plants.

Herbaceous borders However, in the last century the herbaceous border was at last developed as a garden feature. The planting of large borders exclusively with herbaceous perennials, massed in informal drifts of colour, was brought to perfection by Gertrude Jekyll and through her influential books herbaceous borders became major features of many fine Edwardian gardens.

Although glorious at their peak, these sumptuous collections of plants had disadvantages. For well over half the year they offered little of interest, and at some periods they could be highly labour intensive.

Present-day needs Since the last war the interest in gardens has increased rather than diminished but people have smaller gardens where a large, relatively blank area for a good part of the year is unacceptable. There is less time for gardening, too, and getting help is very difficult. For all these reasons there has been a shift away from the pure herbaceous border to mixed borders, in which herbaceous perennials have joined forces with choice shrubs and bulbs in order to give year-round garden interest.

Defining herbaceous perennials In describing plants, gardeners tend to be less strict in their use of words than the scientists whose language they have borrowed. This is true of the term 'herbaceous perennials' and it is worth setting this major category in its broader context.

LEFT *Genista* 'Lydia' and *Geranium* 'Johnson's Blue' effectively banked against stone steps, providing handsome ground cover and leading the eyes upwards.

BELOW In a more subdued but delicately lovely scheme, *G.* 'Johnson's Blue' teamed with pink *G. endressi* used as prolifically flowering ground cover.

Herbaceous plants, unlike trees and shrubs, do not produce woody stems. Annuals and biennials – short-lived plants that die after flowering and setting seed – are strictly speaking herbaceous but the term is commonly restricted to cover those plants that, although not having a permanent woody structure, live on year after year, their life-cycle not brought to an end after they have produced seed to carry on the race. A large number die down in autumn, producing fresh new growth the following year. Others remain evergreen throughout the winter, although with new foliage replacing old on a regular cycle.

Properly speaking, bulbous plants are herbaceous perennials, too, their underground storage organs tiding them over from one season of growth to the next. In practice, however, bulbs and corms are treated as a separate group of garden plants. Under the heading of herbaceous perennials catalogues and garden literature deal with long-lived herbaceous plants such as the bearded irises which have rhizomes and the majority which have fibrous roots.

RIGHT Even in the shade of a tall tree, primroses and *Scilla sibirica* put on a colourful show.

BELOW The showy pink flowers of *Incarvillea arguta* share a sunny spot with *Agapanthus* Headbourne Hybrids.

Herbaceous perennials are also sometimes described as border plants (or perennials) and hardy perennials. The first simply indicates the use to which these plants have been put in the past. But it fails to take into account that many herbaceous plants have uses beyond the traditional border, for instance, as ground-cover under shrubs or as lovely additions to the wild garden.

To describe them as 'hardy' refers to their ability to stand up to winter cold and damp. Hardiness is relative: many plants that are perfectly hardy in most parts of New Zealand, for example, might not survive a European winter, even in southern England.

All of the plants that are described in the following pages should, however, prove hardy in Australia and New Zealand as well as in many parts of Europe, including Great Britain. Although some that are more tender might be grown in pots in the protection of a greenhouse – for example, some of the agapanthus could be treated in this way – these perennials are essentially plants to be grown in the open garden.

PLANTING

Herbaceous perennials are not difficult plants. They can be grown successfully in almost every garden provided that the ground is well prepared in advance, the right plants are chosen for each location and then planted with due care.

A modern herbaceous border in which roses and other flowering shrubs lend their attractions to the display – and extend the flowering season.

Preparing the ground No permanent planting should be put in until you have fully assessed your garden and discovered the strengths and weaknesses of your soil. This is important because, for instance, some plants do not like alkaline soil, of the kind you get in chalky country. However, it is easy to find out whether your soil is acid, alkaline or neutral by using a simple soil-testing kit available from most garden centres. It is best to test soil from several different areas of the garden because very often it differs from one part to another – and that will mean a wider range of plants can be chosen.

A little experimental digging will soon tell you whether your soil is heavy or light and the extent to which it is well drained.

Although suitable plants can be found for almost all types of soil, your chances of growing a wide range of perennials are greatly increased if extreme conditions are modified by careful cultivation. It is worth taking considerable trouble to ensure good drainage. While a boggy garden might suit some plants very well, many of these will also thrive in a moist or well-drained soil in which a wide variety of other plants will also flourish.

All soils are improved by the addition of organic matter. Heavy soils are lightened and made more open, while light soils are given more body and their ability to retain moisture is increased. Among the best organic materials to add to the garden are garden compost, leafmould and farmyard manure. All are rich in nutrients but need to be well rotted before they are dug in. 'Forest Bark' Ground and Composted is easy to manage and will improve the structure of the soil. However, it does not provide the nutrients found in other organic materials and, if this product is used, a general fertilizer should also be added to the soil.

The eradication of perennial weeds is essential if you are to avoid major problems after planting. Digging and mechanical removal will deal satisfactorily with many but some of the most persistent – often multiplied when fragments are distributed by digging and forking – can be treated effectively with modern herbicides. Particularly useful is glyphosate, which kills the complete weed and does not affect the soil.

As a last step in preparation break up any large lumps of soil and add a generous sprinkling of a general fertilizer. Then the ground should be left for several weeks to settle before planting.

When to plant Many garden centres offer a fair range of herbaceous perennials, sold throughout the year as container-grown plants. There are also excellent specialist nurseries who play an important role in keeping the less common plants in commerce and in introducing new plants. They generally send stock out as dormant plants, loose-wrapped, in early autumn. However, orders should be placed well in advance to avoid disappointment.

Dormant perennials are best planted in early autumn but any time between then and spring is satisfactory, provided that the ground is not frozen. Container-grown plants can be put in at any time of the year, although the traditional planting time between autumn and spring generally tends to give the best results.

How to plant Planting is one of the most satisfying jobs in the garden and, provided you begin with sound stock, the success rate with perennials is generally very high. However, careful handling of plants is important because damaged tissue provides an entry point for diseases, and loss of water content in the first critical days after planting

TOP RIGHT To test the pH of your soil, place a couple of teaspoonfuls of soil in a test tube.
TOP FAR RIGHT Carefully pour the acidity-testing solution on to the soil sample.
RIGHT Place the stopper in the neck of the tube, then shake contents to mix.
FAR RIGHT Colour match the resultant solution against the test card. A reading of 6.5-7.0 is best, indicating that the soil is neutral.

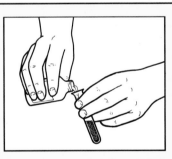

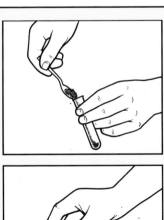

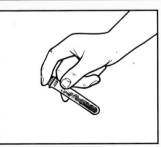

can spell trouble. Particularly when planting perennials that are in leaf, try to plant on cool still days when there is some cloud cover.

Dormant perennials are best planted out as soon as possible after they are received. If planting has to be delayed for several days, remove the plants from their wrappings and store them in a sheltered, shaded spot with moist peat packed around the roots, for example in a clean flowerpot under a hedge or in a cool greenhouse.

Although most perennials can be moved with relative ease in the dormant season – unlike trees and shrubs – it is as well to have marked out where plants are to be positioned, taking into account their potential height and spread. To avoid compacting the soil it is useful to work from a plank that can be moved across the bed as required.

For most plants a trowel will be large enough to dig out a hole sufficient to allow a full spread of the root system. The roots of container-grown plants that have become pot-bound should be carefully loosened but keep the soil ball as complete as possible. In the case of large perennials use a spade to dig out the planting hole and for a plant of any size it is worth adding some moist peat to the planting hole together with a liberal sprinkling of bone-meal and then mixing them both in with the soil.

Set plants at the same depth at which they have already been growing. Many perennials will adjust if set more or less deeply than they have been growing but some may sulk and refuse to flower. Paeonies, in particular, must not be set too deeply when being planted.

Once the plant is at the right depth cover the roots and firm in, leaving the area around the plant

LEFT Small, front of the border plants can be planted with the aid of a trowel.

ABOVE When planting larger, container-grown plants, carefully tease out the roots if they are pot-bound. Depress the soil around plant slightly to help it collect moisture.

ABOVE Fragrant yellow flowers of *Inula hookeri*, teamed with plumy Astilbe tarquetii.

ABOVE RIGHT Twin borders, edging a lawn in traditional style, at Bampton Manor, Oxon.

slightly below the level of the bed surface so that it will collect moisture. Water plants in thoroughly and continue regular watering in dry spells, particularly pot-grown perennials that have been planted out between spring and autumn.

WHERE TO GROW

The adaptability of herbaceous perennials is one of their greatest assets. They can look perfectly at home in a formal garden, their expansiveness softening austere geometry without undermining it. But they are equally at home in quite informal schemes, either on their own, combined with shrubs and bulbs or even forming a constituent of the wild garden.

Herbaceous borders There are still a few large public and private gardens where herbaceous borders can be seen in something approaching their Edwardian splendour. They are generally planted as long rectangles flanking a central path or narrow lawn, each border backed by a wall or hedge. The scale alone is impressive, for a herbaceous border that covered a site under 12 by 3.6m (40 by 12ft) would seem mean.

Within each border the tallest plants, yarrows such as 'Gold Plate' or delphiniums, stand tall at the back, with below them groups of other perennials ranked according to height.

What, according to all accounts, made Gertrude Jekyll's planting of herbaceous borders so remarkable was the artistry with which she massed perennials to create subtle drifts and great climaxes of colour. She always began by putting her planting schemes on paper. Anyone with the means and leisure to create a modern herbaceous border should begin in the same way, plotting out to scale groups of plants arranged according to height and colour and taking into account the time of their flowering. Planning in this way will give the maximum effect over a prolonged season.

In laying out a border it is helpful to leave a narrow path between the back of it and the wall or hedge

LEFT An undulating path of crazy paving softened by lavish plantings of perennials which also conceal its further progress.

RIGHT Spectacular rich red autumnal colouring of *Bergenia cordifolia* – a prized front of border plant.

BELOW A small island bed housing shrubs and herbaceous perennials.

behind in order to provide easy access when work has to be done. Considerable labour is involved in maintaining a large, traditional herbaceous border – staking and deadheading as well as manuring and weeding – and anything that helps to make the tasks easier is welcome. Furthermore, the proximity of a wall or hedge tends to draw moisture from the soil, encouraging lank floppy growth close by. But if given a little space plants will grow in a more naturally upright manner.

Island beds Another approach to growing herbaceous perennials, particularly suitable for large informal gardens, is to group them in island beds. In contrast to the conventional border backed by a wall or hedge these are generally of irregular shape, perhaps 3.6m (12ft) or more across at the widest point, and set in a lawn so that they can be approached and viewed from all sides. A forced regularity is out of place in this kind of bed but the tallest plants should be positioned near the centre and there should be a downwards gradation of plant heights all round this central point.

The fact that island beds can be seen from all sides may be an advantage visually, but the effect will clearly depend on careful grouping of plants. For the gardener a major advantage is that access on all sides makes maintenance much easier. It is also generally true that in a good open position, provided perennials have been adequately spaced, they will grow to their natural height and not get drawn and lanky as they sometimes do in traditional borders. In smaller gardens it is certainly worth while experimenting with

miniature island beds but planting must always be kept in scale.

Mixed borders For most gardeners interested in growing a wide range of plants but with a limited amount of time to devote to gardening, one of the best solutions is to use herbaceous perennials in mixed borders. Within a garden of formal design these beds or borders can be geometric in shape but in an informal layout they can be given an irregular outline.

There may be one or two small trees casting dappled shade, a backbone of large shrubs and then a mixture of smaller shrubs and herbaceous perennials. To these can be added bulbs, valuable at all seasons but especially welcome in spring for their wonderfully fresh colours. If bulbs are included, they should be planted deep so that they are not damaged when beds are dug over. It is a good idea to keep a note of which bulbs are planted where, so that you can exercise extra care when you happen to be digging in those areas.

When planting shrubs in mixed borders account should be taken of the shade they cast. The choice of perennials for mixed borders is almost umlimited but much work can be saved by choosing sturdy plants that require a minimum of staking, including short-growing varieties of border favourites such as achilleas, bearded irises and oriental poppies.

Groundcover Although for many of us, much of the pleasure of a garden is derived from working in it, even the most devoted gardeners usually have limited time for general maintenance, but there are time-saving ploys.

Among the most trouble-free ways of dealing with areas of the garden that are not main focal points is to plant them with shrubs underplanted with vigorous clumpforming and spreading herbaceous perennials. Provided the ground has been thoroughly cleared of perennial weeds in advance, the best of these – including alchemilla, bergenias and many of the geraniums – will make a dense growth of attractive foliage, often with the bonus of beautiful flowers, yet without becoming too seriously invasive. The principle can be applied on almost any scale, including small town gardens that otherwise might be totally neglected or else covered in paving.

Wild gardens offer another appealing way of growing many herbaceous perennials. The great advocate of natural planting was William Robinson, one of most prolific gardening writers of the late nineteenth and early twentieth centuries. His ideas, so passionately held, have again found favour in a period when conservation issues are constantly before us.

It needs to be stressed that wild gardening does involve a degree of management if a happy combination of well-behaved native plants and vigorous easy-going introductions is to be maintained without bullying weeds taking over. At its best, however, the wild garden in which flourishing plants do not betray the gardener's hand can sometimes be of quite breath-taking beauty. And it is becoming increasingly popular.

A group of two or three trees, even part of an old orchard, can be transformed into a glade where many natural woodlanders, including Solomon's seal, hostas and some of the geraniums, will provide a perfect underplanting. The edge of a pond is another area that could be treated in a comparably free way, with bold-leaved rheums mixed with other moisture-loving plants such as trollius and astilbes.

Rock gardens and raised beds Many alpines and rock-garden plants are simply dwarf herbaceous perennials, most of them under 45cm (1½ft) in height. Their small-scale charm is undeniable but a rock garden containing exclusively dwarf plants can appear curiously dull as a feature in the garden. A few of the larger herbaceous perennials such as euphorbias and paeonies combined with a few shrubs such as

BELOW FAR LEFT
A raised bed brings
a display of dwarf
perennials into greater
prominence.

RIGHT Variegated
hostas lend interest to
a shady patio and the
container can be
moved at will.

BELOW Lilies make
highly attractive patio
plants when in flower,
and they appreciate a
sheltered spot.

Containers Herbaceous perennials are generally thought of as plants for the open garden but some are very effective grown in containers and there is certainly scope for experimenting with others. The taller hostas make magnificent clumps for large pots and these can provide impressive focal points in shady areas of the garden. Equally impressive in full sun are the 'Headbourne Hybrids' of *Agapanthus*, with their large heads of blue flowers above glossy green leaves.

The one point that the adventurous gardener must remember when growing herbaceous perennials in containers is that regular watering is essential. They dry out remarkably quickly, particularly in hot sun. The best time for watering is in the cool of early evening.

dwarf maples and hebes can provide background and accents against which dwarf plants are seen to better effect.

Raised beds are an attractive way of growing a collection of small herbaceous perennials such as pinks, pulsatillas and some of the companulas and dwarf shrubs, including daphnes and dwarf conifers. A bed 45-60cm (1½-2ft) high brings the plants closer to the eye and makes maintenance very much easier. Larger perennials can also be grown in raised beds, which provide one of the best ways of allowing those with disabilities to participate actively in tending their garden.

Also, make sure that the container has good drainage holes and put a thick layer of crocks in the base, topped by a layer of peat, before planting the perennials in good compost. Waterlogged plants fare no better than dried-out ones.

It is a good idea, too, to give a foliar feed from time to time, adhering to the manufacturer's recommendation for this. Make a point of always reading the label carefully.

GENERAL CARE

As a group herbaceous perennials are not especially demanding plants and general good garden practice will meet most of their requirements. To perform well they need an adequate supply of water, nutrients that will produce healthy growth and freedom from weed competition.

An established herbaceous border in full flower is a marvellous sight, but only for as long as it is properly tended in terms of staking, feeding and dead-heading – and generally kept under control.

Weed control Many weeds can be easily removed by hand or loosened by carefully working a hoe or cultivator through beds. It is especially important to clear beds at the start of the growing season and this is a time, too, when the surface of the ground should be loosened.

Deep-rooted perennials, such as bindweed, that get established among herbaceous perennials are more troublesome. Apply a spot weedkiller, such as one of those containing glyphosate, to the leaves and repeat if necessary.

Feeding and mulching The application of slow-acting fertilizers in early spring will promote strong growth. A general compound fertilizer, such as Rose 'Plus', can be used or alternatively a mixture of the organic fertilizers bonemeal and

hoof and horn. On poor soils it may be worth supplementing this feed between early and mid-summer with one or two applications of a quick-acting fertilizer applied as a foliar spray.

A mulch of organic material such as 'Forest Bark' Ground and Composted Bark or rotted compost, provides plants with nutrients, helps conserve moisture and discourages the germination of weeds. The best time to mulch is from mid- to late spring immediately after beds have been throughly weeded. At this time of the year the ground is normally still quite moist but, if the weather is dry, it is important to water before mulching. Apply the mulch thickly, to a depth of about 7.5cm (3in). Perennials in mulched beds will not need watering unless there is an exceptional period of dry weather.

Staking A complaint levelled against some tall perennials is that they need staking or some other support, otherwise they will flop over or get damaged by wind. In old gardens with herbaceous borders it was taken for granted that there would be labour available for this and other chores.

Much of the trouble of staking and supporting can be avoided by growing sturdy varieties of medium rather than tall growth and by positioning beds in sheltered parts of the garden. With some plants, however, some kind of support may be necessary and what is needed is a method that is effective and yet at the same time not conspicuous.

Various kinds of frames are available commercially which can be set over plants as they come into growth, giving solidity and support where needed without being obvious at the height of the season.

A traditional alternative is the use of pea sticks, twiggy branches up to about 90cm (3ft) high, which are carefully inserted into the centre of clumps as they come into leaf. At a point below the eventual height of the perennial bend the ends of these branches over towards the centre and intermesh them to increase the firmness of this simple frame.

With heavier plants the support may need to be in the form of canes strategically placed around a plant or group of plants with twine tied round. Tall single-stemmed plants, such as delphiniums, can be tied to bamboo canes carefully inserted close to the plant.

With all these supports it is important that they are put in place early in the growing season, when there is no risk of damaging the plant in the process. Once growth gets under way they will quickly be hidden by an abundance of foliage.

Several unobtrusive forms of commercially available staking have been used in this border but you can also easily make your own from pea sticks or canes and garden twine.

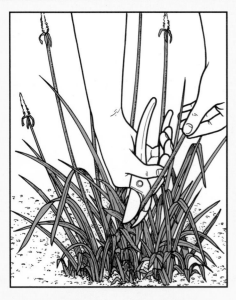

Removing unsightly dead flowers tidies up beds and borders, and induces a second flowering in some perennials, such as lupins.

ABOVE When the flowers of plants with bare stems fade, cut them right down to the base.

ABOVE RIGHT If the lower stem bears foliage, cut back to the top leaves.

RIGHT *Sedum spectabile* is among those perennials whose attractive flowerheads can be left over winter, to lend a spot of colour to the garden.

Tidying up Deadheading all perennials in the garden in the second half of summer could be a major job and it is only worth dealing with those that are unsightly. Straggly foliage and stems can be trimmed at the same time. However, some perennials that flower early, such as lupins and delphiniums, if deadheaded as soon as flowers fade, may then produce secondary flower spikes later in the summer.

In autumn dead and dying stems and leaves can be cut back but some plants, including deciduous epimediums and astilbes, are an attractive russet colour in the winter garden and these can be left until early spring. In particularly cold areas the crowns of the more tender perennials can be protected by covering them with the cut-down top growth.

Plant renewal Although some perennials are very long-lived, others will need to be lifted and divided after several years. For appropriate methods to follow, please see the section on propagation, pages 24-27.

THROUGH THE YEAR

March Primroses, Lenten roses, bergenias, euphorbias and pulmonarias add their own fresh beauty to that of spring bulbs. Complete main planting and propagation by division. Clear borders and apply a general fertilizer.

April The Pasque flower, the flower of Easter, makes a lovely addition to the perennials of early spring. Complete clearing ground and then add a liberal mulch of organic material. Begin staking and supporting plants as they come into growth. Outdoor sowings of perennials can begin. Take basal cuttings of plants such as lupins and delphiniums.

May Classics of the herbaceous border – bearded irises, lupins, paeonies and oriental poppies – come into flower as spring slips into summer. Ensure support for flopping and tall plants. If necessary, begin a regular programme of spraying to control aphids (see page 28).

ABOVE The pasque flower, *Pulsatilla vulgaris*, has finely-cut foliage and cup-shaped flowers. There are both pink and red varieties as well as the purple type.

LEFT Mixed lupins in full flower make a very colourful display in early summer and are ideal plants for either beds or borders.

Papaver orientale comes into flower in late May or early June, the rich scarlet flowers with their characteristic black blotch making a spectacular show. Cut them back in July.

June Most herbaceous perennials will now be in full leaf and the long summer pageant begins. Star performers include tall delphiniums, paeonies and, on a smaller scale, deliciously scented pinks. As the flower spikes of lupins and delphiniums begin to go over cut them back. Divide bearded irises.

July In many gardens mid-summer is the climax of the flowering year, with a wide variety of plants in full bloom. In dry weather water thoroughly. Cut back early-flowering perennials such as oriental poppies.

August For a few weeks the glory of the summer garden remains at its peak, sustained by late-season flowers such as phlox and Japanese anemones. Continue to water when necessary. Where practicable deadhead flowers that have faded.

September In a good year summer-flowering perennials may continue well into autumn but the plants of the season – asters, Japanese anemones and phlox – take centre stage. The new main planting season can begin while the ground is still warm.

Take cuttings of sub-shrubby perennials such as artemisia.

October Bees and butterflies make the most of late flowers such as *Sedum* 'Autumn Joy' but already the yellow and tawny colours of dying leaves, clear yellow in the case of many hostas, are the dominant colours of the flower garden. Cut back untidy dead leaves and stems, using cut material to cover the crowns of more tender perennials. Begin lifting and dividing plants that are showing signs of loss of vigour and begin propagation from root cuttings.

November The collapse of most deciduous perennials is almost complete but some, the astilbes and epimediums among them, have beautifully tawny leaves that are of value in the winter garden. Continue main planting and propagation by division and root cuttings.

December Evergreen stalwarts of the flower garden such as bergenias and hellebores are easily overlooked during the height of summer but come into their own in winter. Avoid planting while there is risk of frosty and snowy weather during winter and early spring.

January A few hardy perennials, including the Christmas rose and stinking hellebore, brave the coldest weather to companion the earliest spring bulbs. Begin sowing seed under glass.

February Hellebores remain the dominant flowering perennials of the coldest months, with Lenten roses taking over from Christmas roses. Clear away any dead foliage left over the winter months.

ABOVE *Sedum* 'Autumn Joy' is justly one of the favourite, late-flowering plants, valued not only for its clusters of tiny flowers but for its attractive leaves and stems. It is a favourite of bees and butterflies, too.

LEFT *Anemone japonica* is another good autumn flowering plant. Afterwards, cut down the stems to ground level.

PROPAGATION

Despite what some less experienced gardeners might think, the flowering of plants is not an end in itself. It is just one stage in the reproductive cycle that leads to the production of viable seed that will eventually germinate to form a new generation of plants; self-propagation, in fact. Of course there are other good ways to improve your stock, as this chapter will describe.

LEFT *Phlox* 'Norah Leigh', *Salvia superba* and *Ligularia przewalskii.* All are easily propagated – in the case of the phlox by stem cuttings and the latter two by division.

RIGHT *Paeonia* 'Rose Garland'. Paeonies are slow to flower but well worth the wait. Keep in a nursery bed for three years for best results.

Herbaceous perennials are like other plants in the way they grow from seed and yet gardeners generally begin by planting young stock rather than by sowing seed. There are two reasons for this. The first is a matter of the time it takes for some perennials to reach flowering size. Growing plants from seed is a challenge but not a speedy way to stock a garden. The second concerns the quality of stock that can be raised from seed.

The pollination and germination of flowers in the wild generally produces populations of relatively uniform character. However, so often the plants gardeners grow are selected forms or hybrids with characteristics that are only perpetuated if stocks are propagated vegetatively, by dividing up or taking cuttings from a parent plant. Selected plants will sometimes come true from seed but only when pollination is controlled. Seed for growing herbaceous perennials must, therefore, come from a reliable source for predictable results.

As long as these points are understood it can still be worth growing plants from seed, either buying from a reputable seed supplier or risking uneven results from seed collected in the garden. Lenten roses provide a good example of plants that can be expensive to buy but where pollination in a mixed planting may give a very interesting range of seedlings.

From seed In the case of easy plants such as *Campanula persicifolia* sow in a prepared bed in the open garden from mid-spring into summer. In the case of many perennials,

however, better results are achieved by sowing under glass from mid-winter to early spring. For indoor sowing use a John Innes or peat-based seed compost in a tray or pot, making sure the compost has been thoroughly watered and then allowed to drain through before sowing. Distribute the seeds evenly, covering all but the finest with a light layer of compost.

Trays or pots, covered with a polythene bag to keep up moisture content and temperature, can be kept inside, in a cold frame or in a greenhouse. Remove the polythene cover as soon as seeds begin to germinate, which may take several weeks, even months.

When two true leaves show, prick out seedlings into containers filled with potting compost and gradually harden plants off in a cold frame before planting out in a nursery bed in the garden. Plants can be moved to permanent positions between autumn and early spring.

Some perennials, including aqui-legias, hellebores, paeonies and the pulsatillas, germinate most freely if subjected to a period of chilling. Sow ripe seed outdoors in autumn, making sure the seeds are protected from birds. Paeonies take two years to show the first leaf. They and some hellebores, such as Christmas and Lenten roses, are slow to come into flowering and are best kept in the nursery bed for three years before being planted out in the open.

Division A more common way of increasing stocks of herbaceous perennials is by division, a method that ensures that the characteristics of the parent plants are perpetuated. Many fibrous-rooted perennials, including phlox, achilleas, gera-niums and *Monarda didyma* tend to become congested at the centre and the best way of maintaining vigor-ous free-flowering stock is to lift and divide plants after several years. Lift old clumps in mild weather between autumn and early spring.

Begin by dividing the clump into four, if necessary prising it apart using two garden forks back to back.

25

Divide bergenias every three years.

roots to each. Smaller, less matted perennials and those with fleshy roots, such as agapanthus, can generally be pulled apart by hand. Others, including rheums, form a woody crown and this is best divided using a sharp knife. Plant the divisions immediately into prepared ground, to which should be added a sprinkled handful of bonemeal, and water in well.

A number of perennials with thick fleshy rhizomes, bergenias and bearded irises being two examples, often need division every three to five years. Bergenias are best divided in early spring, young rhizomes with strong growth buds and healthy roots being cut away from the old rhizome, which can be discarded. Clean up the rhizome, removing any dead leaves or damaged parts, before planting them in the way described above and at

Then discard the tough central part and any damaged roots. If still large, the healthy and vigorous remaining sections can be divided further into pieces with five or six buds as well as

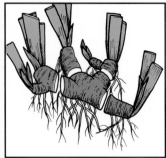

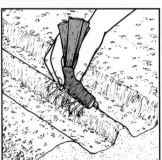

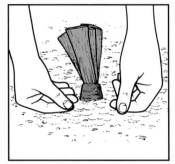

TOP FAR LEFT To propagate bearded irises, lift out a clump with five or more pairs of leaves.

TOP LEFT Trim back the leaves by half, then cut plant into separate rhizomes.

BELOW FAR LEFT Set each rhizome on a low ridge, with the roots spread out.

BELOW LEFT Firm in the soil around the roots and lower part of rhizome but leave the top exposed as shown.

Paeonies can be divided, too.

The use of a hormone rooting powder generally promotes rapid root development. Make a hole with a dibber and insert the cuttings in individual pots containing a cuttings compost or equal parts mixed of peat and sand. Keep well-watered in a closed frame, gradually increasing ventilation when new growth begins to show. After six to eight weeks repot in a standard potting compost and grow on before planting out in the garden in the autumn.

A few sub-shrubby perennials, such as artemisias, can be grown from cuttings taken in early autumn from the tips of vigorous non-flowering stems. Insert in a cuttings compost or a mixture of equal parts of peat and sand, covering the top of the pot with clear polythene, and ensuring that it does not touch the cuttings, to maintain a close atmosphere. After about six weeks, when cuttings have taken, repot individually in a potting compost and keep these new plants in a cold frame over winter.

the same depth as the parent plant.

Bearded irises are best dealt with after flowering. Each young rhizome cut from the old plant should have at least one good leaf fan. When replanting leave the top of the rhizome showing and trim the leaves by about one half.

Paeonies are long-lived and therefore do not normally need lifting and division, plants continuing to flower freely over decades if regularly fed and mulched. However, the woody rootstocks can be lifted in the autumn and divided by cutting so that each portion has several growth buds. Do not plant more deeply than the parent. Paeonies grown from divisions may take a year or two to come into flowering.

From cuttings A number of relatively short-lived perennials, such as delphiniums and lupins, are best propagated from basal cuttings taken in spring. Cut the young shoots off cleanly from low down.

Root cuttings Many perennials are easily propagated from root cuttings taken between autumn and early spring. In the case of those with thick roots, such as oriental poppies, take portions about 7.5cm (3in) in length and insert them vertically in pots containing a mixture of equal parts of peat and sand or a potting compost. In the case of those with thinner roots, such as phlox, take cuttings about 5cm (2in) long and lay them horizontally, just covered by the compost or peat and sand mixture. After cuttings have spent a winter in a closed frame they should begin to shoot and then they can be potted up individually in a potting compost. Leave pots in the open during the summer and plant out in permanent positions in the autumn.

PESTS AND DISEASES

In a well-managed garden the disorders that can trouble herbaceous perennials are not generally a major problem. To minimize the risk of attack from pests and diseases plant on well-cultivated ground and choose plants appropriate to the conditions. If you then ensure an adequate supply of nutrients and water and keep weeds under control, plants have the best possible chance of making sturdy healthy growth.

When problems do arise they can often be dealt with effectively using the wide range of chemical pesticides available to the gardener. These must, however, be properly handled and should be carefully stored where children cannot reach them. Read the instructions carefully before buying a product to ensure that it is the correct one for the job, and always apply the treatment as instructed.

PESTS

Aphids Of the number of pests that weaken their hosts by sucking sap from them aphids are the most troublesome. Also known as greenfly and blackfly, they attack a wide range of plants and in summer months multiply at a prodigious rate if not checked. In the process of taking sap they may also transmit viruses and for this reason alone

Snail with eggs.

their control is important. The use of an insecticide such as 'Rapid' or 'Sybol' applied about every ten days during the growing season, will keep infestations under control.

Caterpillars Leaf and flower damage can be caused by caterpillars and a number of insects. In some cases pests can be removed by hand

Aphid damage on lupins.

and sometimes the level of damage is tolerable. If control is necessary, use a general insecticide such as 'Sybol' applied as a spray or in dust form.

Phlox eelworm A few plants have pests that are specific to them. Phlox eelworm, for example, can seriously weaken phlox plants, causing the leaves to die off prematurely.

28

Caterpillar feeding on chrysanthemum.

Affected plants should be burned and any replacement stock should be put in a different area of the garden, where the soil has not been infected.

Rabbits In areas where these are a problem it may be necessary to enclose all or part of the garden with a rabbit-proof fence.

Slugs and snails are in the first rank of destructive pests, especially on heavy soils, and are most active in mild damp weather. They show a marked relish for certain herbaceous perennials, including delphiniums and hostas.

Baits containing metaldehyde, such as ICI Mini Slug Pellets, provide a reasonably effective control. In the case of vulnerable plants, do not wait until there are evident signs of damage before you start laying baits – otherwise it could very well prove too late.

Swift moth caterpillars The underground parts of herbaceous plants can also be attacked by pests, such as swift moth caterpillars, that feed on the roots. These are best controlled by the application of an insecticide such as 'Sybol' used as a drench for existing infestations or as a dust to prevent attack.

DISEASES

Although all plants can be affected by viral diseases, causing yellowing, striping and blotching of leaves, these are not generally a major problem of herbaceous perennials. However, there is no satisfactory chemical treatment if an outbreak does occur, so all infected plants should be burned.

Rusts, mildews and other fungus diseases. *Rusts* show in distorted growth and orange-yellow spore pustules; *mildews* show as a powdery coating on leaves and stems. A very wide range of symptoms and damage can result from *disease* attack, such as leaf spots (which themselves may be caused by a wide variety of fungi), grey mould, wilt and rots. Remove the infected part of the plant before the problem can spread. If you do need to take further controlling measures, use a general systemic fungicide such as 'Nimrod'-T or Benlate + 'Activex' 2. In their mildest forms fungal diseases disfigure plants and weaken them. The more serious moulds cause rotting and bring about the total collapse of the plant. If fungal infections are not promptly dealt with, there is a strong likelihood of them spreading to other plants close by.

Fungi may be specific to a particular group of plants: rhizome rot, for example, attacks rhizomatous irises and paeony wilt attacks paeonies. Plants seriously damaged by disease should be dug up and burned. Where disease damage is less severe the affected part can be cut out and the plant treated with a general fungicide such as Benlate + 'Activex' 2. Plants in the general vicinity and the ground from which infected plants have been taken should also be treated.

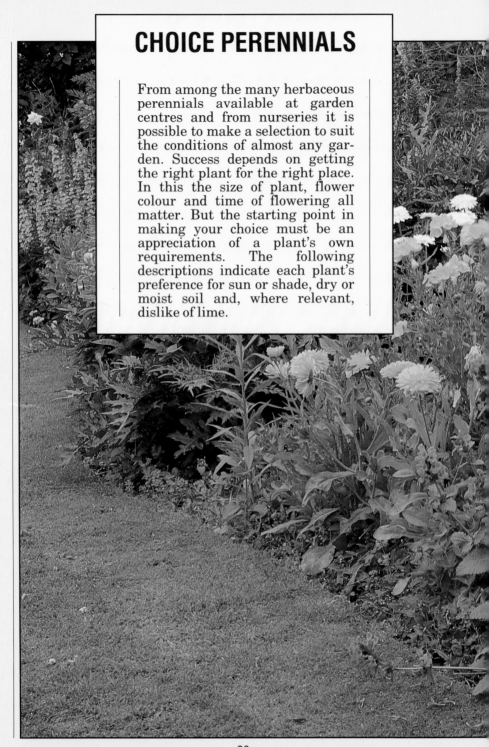

CHOICE PERENNIALS

From among the many herbaceous perennials available at garden centres and from nurseries it is possible to make a selection to suit the conditions of almost any garden. Success depends on getting the right plant for the right place. In this the size of plant, flower colour and time of flowering all matter. But the starting point in making your choice must be an appreciation of a plant's own requirements. The following descriptions indicate each plant's preference for sun or shade, dry or moist soil and, where relevant, dislike of lime.

Acanthus

(Bear's breeches) The glossy deep green leaves of *A. spinosus*, which are deeply cut and spiny, form an imposing base about 90cm (3ft) across. The long-lasting flower spikes emerge in mid-summer to make a statuesque plant 90-120cm (4-5ft) high. Green bracts fringe the tubular, purple and white flowers. This species thrives in dry, even alkaline, soil, in sun or light shade. *A. mollis*, with broader, less cut leaves, likes good, well-drained soil.

Achillea

(Yarrow) For a season of 6-8 weeks starting in early summer the fine hybrid 'Moonshine' carries flat heads of cool yellow flowers. They stand about 60cm (2ft) above the feathery grey-green foliage, which persists throughout winter. In the larger garden, varieties of *A. filipendulina* can make a bold display if planted in groups. The broad heads of 'Gold Plate', one of the best, are borne on stems 1.2-1.5m (4-5ft) high. Yarrows need well-drained soil on a site in full sun.

Aconitum

(Monkshood) The species and hybrids of monkshood are valuable for their tall stems of hooded flowers borne above attractively cut leaves, generally in the second half of summer and early autumn. 'Bressingham Spire', which grows to 90cm (3ft), has violet-blue flowers. 'Bicolor', almost as tall, combines this shade with white. 'Kelmscott' is a rich blue form of the species *A. carmichaelii*. All do well in sun or shade but prefer deep moist soil. All parts of the plants are poisonous.

Acanthus spinosus

Achillea filipendula 'Gold Plate'

Ajuga reptans 'Burgundy Glow' makes admirable ground cover

Agapanthus

(African lily) For a long season, beginning in mid-summer, the 'Headbourne Hybrids' carry flowers predominantly in shades of blue but also in white. The flower stems are about 60cm (2ft) high and they rise from a base of dark green strap-shaped leaves. These are reasonably hardy plants but are at their best when planted in a sunny sheltered position with well-drained soil.

Ajuga reptans

(Bugle) Several forms of this woodland plant have been selected for the colouring of their evergreen ground-covering leaves. 'Purpurea' has burnished purple leaves, while 'Burgundy Glow' has a cream edge setting off deep wine shades. Blue flowers are carried on stubby spikes about 20cm (8in) high in late spring and early summer. Bugles tolerate a wide range of conditions but leaf colouring is best when they are grown in moist soil on a site that is in light shade.

Alchemilla mollis

(Lady's mantle) Few plants as easy-going as lady's mantle can match it for beauty. Throughout summer there are loose sprays of small greenish-yellow flowers above mounds 45cm (1½ft) high of velvety light green leaves. Lady's mantle prefers moist but not boggy soil in sun or light shade. It self-seeds freely (but any unwanted seedlings are easily removed).

Alstroemeria

(Peruvian lily) In the second half of summer the showy heads of lily-like flowers are attractive in the garden or for cutting. The 'Ligtu Hybrids', in shades of orange and pink, grow to about 75cm (2½ft) and are reasonably hardy. However, they need a sunny position and well-drained soil. The roots are brittle so plants need careful handling and may take a year or two to settle after planting. A strong family resemblance can be seen in *A. aurantiaca*, but this can spread vigorously.

Artemisia absinthium

Anemone × hybrida

(Japanese anemone) In late summer and autumn the Japanese anemones provide a long season of beautiful flowers borne elegantly above dark green leaves. They tolerate shade but flower better in sun and thrive in ordinary moisture-retentive soil, to the point of becoming invasive. Among excellent old hybrids, growing to 1.5m (5ft), are the single white 'Honorine Jobert' and the semi-double pink 'Queen Charlotte'. 'Bressingham Glow', a more recent variety, is shorter and has rosy red semi-double flowers.

Aquilegia vulgaris

(Granny's bonnet, columbine) This pretty plant has grey-green divided leaves and short-spurred, blue, white or pink flowers. Several hybrid strains offer a broader colour range and in many the spurs are elegantly lengthened. The 'McKana Hybrids' grow to 90cm (3ft) and have brightly coloured flowers with fine tapering spurs. Aquilegias are easy plants in ordinary soil, and thrive in sun or light shade.

Artemisia

(Wormwood) Many of the artemisias can be a nuisance, spreading by running roots, but the common wormwood, *A. absinthium*, is well behaved. In the form 'Lambrook Silver' it makes a fine foliage plant about 75cm (2½ft) tall with feathery silver-grey leaves. In the second half of summer there are small yellow flowers. For a dome of silver filigree only 10cm (4in) high try *A. schmidtiana* 'Nana'. Like most of the artemisias, both of these revel in sun and well-drained, even dry poor soil.

Aster

The true Michaelmas daises are the numerous varieties of *A. novi-belgii*, attractive plants in a wide range of flower colours but prone to mildew and in other respects not trouble free. A similar but more dependable plant is *A. × frikartii*, which flowers from mid-summer to mid-autumn, just when the garden is in need of sustained colour. The flowers are lavender blue with a yellow centre, particularly good in the form 'Mönch', and are borne with great freedom on plants about 90cm (3ft) high. Plant in groups, in sunny positions where there is well-drained soil.

Aster novi-belgii

Astilbe

The hybrid astilbes, like their parents, are moisture-loving plants that do best in light shade. They are interesting over a long period, their ferny leaves, often tinted bronze, topped in summer by fluffy plumes or, in some varieties, by more erect and denser spires of tiny flowers. Throughout winter the dead stems and flowers remain a warm russet. Among the taller varieties, which can measure between 60/90cm (2-3ft) high, 'Fanal' and 'Red Sentinel' are crimson red, 'Snowdrift' and 'Deutschland' are white, and 'Bressingham Beauty' is pink. The shell-pink 'Sprite', which grows to about 30cm (1ft), is an outstanding dwarf hybrid.

Astrantia major

(Masterwort) *A. major* makes a good clump of attractive foliage, above which stems about 45cm (1½ft) tall carry heads of curious starry flowers, greenish white at the centre and surrounded by a green collar. The cool quiet beauty of their flowering season lasts for 6-8 weeks, plants performing well in ordinary soil in sun or light shade. *A.m.* 'Rubra' has a plum-red collar.

Bergenia

Tolerating a wide range of conditions and thriving in sun or shade, bergenias are useful evergreen ground cover with the bonus of dense flowerheads in spring. The broad leathery leaves of many take on attractive red tones in autumn and winter. Among those that colour well are *B. cordifolia* 'Purpurea', about 60cm (2ft) high, and *B. purpurascens*, to about 30cm (1ft), both with magenta-pink flowers. Good hybrids include: 'Abendglut' ('Evening Glow'), only 25cm (10in) high, colouring to deepest red and with purplish flowers; 'Ballawley', with crimson flowers; and 'Silberlicht' ('Silver Light'), with white flowers that become pinkish with age.

Astilbe arendsii 'Fanal'

Astrantia major

Brunnera

After sending out loose sprays of blue forget-me-not flowers in late spring and early summer *B. macrophylla* makes a good foliage plant, producing large heart-shaped leaves throughout summer. The rough-textured leaves form clumps about 45cm (1½ft) high. An excellent plant for shady borders and as underplanting for trees and shrubs.

Campanula lactiflora

(Bellflower) Among the best in a genus containing many good plants, the giant bellflower carries full heads of starry blue flowers. Best planted in groups of three or more, allowing 45cm (1½ft) between plants, it will make an impressive clump up to 1.5m (5ft) high. It is happy with ordinary soil in sun or light shade. 'Pritchard's Variety' has deep blue flowers while 'Loddon Anna' is pale pink.

Campanula lactiflora

C. persicifolia

(Peach-leaved bellflower) The narrow evergreen leaves form a tight rosette from which the flower stems grow to 90-120cm (3-4ft). The bell-shaped flowers, borne over a long season in summer if plants are regularly deadheaded, are blue or white. 'Telham Beauty' has particularly large deep blue flowers. Easily pleased in sun or shade, and self-seeding freely.

Chrsyanthemum

(Shasta daisy) For many weeks in mid-summer the Shasta daisies, *C. maximum*, make mounds up to 90cm (3ft) high of rayed white flowers. Several named forms, including doubles such as 'Wirral Supreme', are all good in the garden and for cutting. These plants do well in ordinary soil in full sun but they need watering in long dry periods.

Chrysanthemum maximum

36

Delphinium

LARGE FLOWERED HYBRIDS

Delphiniums are classic plants of the mid-summer herbaceous border, their great spires of flowers rising above pale green, deeply cut leaves, sometimes to a height of more than 1.8m (6ft). The colour range includes not only every shade of blue but white, yellow, pink, purple and, a recent introduction, red.

These showy plants are not for the lazy gardener. They need good soil and full sun, are not long-lived and, like many highly bred plants, they are prone to attack from pests and diseases, slugs being particularly troublesome. Furthermore the stems need staking. When well grown, however, they are among the most splendid plants of the flower garden.

BELLADONNA HYBRIDS

More manageable, though less magnificent, than the large-flowered hybrids, these are shorter plants that grow to 1.2m (4½ft), with less densely packed flowers. If spent spikes are removed promptly, it is possible to keep the flowering season going from mid-summer to autumn. They, too, need good soil and sun, and protection from slugs.

Delphinium hybrid 'Honey Bee'

Dianthus 'Inchmery'

Dianthus

MODERN PINKS

These are charming plants for the front of a border, generally under 40cm (16in) in height. The grassy leaves are grey-green and the flowers are borne freely in early and mid-summer, often with a second flush in the autumn. They are hybrids, descended from *D. × allwoodii*, including reliable plants such as the deliciously scented 'Doris', with double salmon-pink flowers. They need gritty well-drained ground and do well in limy soils.

OLD-FASHIONED PINKS

Few plants are as evocative of cottage gardens as the old-fashioned pinks. Many have beautifully laced flowers and almost all are heavily scented. They require the same conditions as modern pinks but need less frequent propagation – about every four or five years. Generally they flower once only, in early summer. 'Inchmery' is a soft pink, while the equally popular 'Mrs Sinkins' is a very full white; among the laced, 'Dad's Favourite' is purple on white.

Dicentra

(Bleeding heart) Several popular names are descriptive of the pendulous red flowers of *D. spectabilis*. These are borne on arching stems in late spring and early summer over ferny grey-green leaves on an exceptionally graceful plant standing up to 75cm (2½ft). Choose a sheltered position in sun or light shade, incorporating some fresh compost in the soil. The white form, 'Alba', is of comparable beauty.

A shorter species, *D. formosana*, to 45cm (1½ft), has more finely cut leaves but similar locket-shaped flowers; 'Adrian Bloom' is a good crimson variety to seek out.

Echinops ritro

Echinops

(Globe thistle) Provided it has sun, even on poor soils *E. ritro* makes a handsome base of jagged silver and green leaves. Above these, tall grey stems carry round prickly flowerheads to a height of 1.2m (4ft). The flowers are about 5cm (2in) across, changing from metallic blue to mauve when they open in late summer. If you want to use them in dried-flower arrangements, cut before the flowers are fully open.

Epimedium

The epimediums are ground-cover plants of quality, their heart-shaped leaves, often beautifully tinted, carried elegantly on fine stems. Even deciduous kinds, such as *E. × rubrum*, retain their leaves throughout the winter. This hybrid, which grows to about 30cm (1ft), has particularly fine bronze tints when young and in autumn the leaves turn orange and gold. In mid-spring there are sprays of small crimson flowers.

Other epimediums to look for are *E. perralderanum*, which is evergreen, and *E. × versicolor* 'Sulphureum', both with yellow flowers. All will do well in either sun or shade and are happy in ordinary soil.

Eryngium

Flower arrangers love the jagged beauty of eryngiums, which in many species have beautifully coloured stems and flowerheads. Among the finest is *E. bourgatii*. It grows to 60cm (2ft) and in summer the wiry branching stems carry silvery blue thistle flowers set in spiky bracts. Other striking plants include *E. alpinum* and *E. × oliverianum*. Like *E. bourgatii*, these thrive in sunny positions where there are well-drained, even dry, soils.

Eryngium alpinum

Euphorbia c. wulfenii 'Lambrook Gold'

Euphorbia

(Spurge) Although the perennial euphorbias have insignificant flowers, the showy bracts surrounding these last for many weeks and the plants are often attractive on account of their foliage. Throughout spring *E. polychroma* makes a greenish-yellow dome about 45cm (1½ft) high. The evergreen *E. characias* and its subspecies *E. c. wulfenii* hold their flowerheads for months from early spring, and make substantial clumps up to 1.2m (4ft) tall. They do well even in quite poor soils in sun or light shade.

Gentiana

(Willow gentian) Many gentians are for the rock garden or alpine house but *G. asclepiadea* is a plant for shady borders or for growing among shrubs in deep moist soil. Its common name refers to the arching willow-like leaves, carried on stems 60cm (2ft) high. Blue or white flowers are carried in pairs along the stems from mid-summer.

Geranium

(Cranesbill) As ground cover the larger cranesbills are almost unequalled, making dense clumps of very attractively divided leaves. Many also flower over a long season. They do well in ordinary soil, whether sited in sun or light shade.

A vigorous evergreen species, *G. endressii*, is rarely without a few pink flowers from late spring to autumn. Good forms include the silvery-pink 'A.T. Johnson' and the bright 'Wargrave Pink'. These all grow to about 75cm (1½ft). 'Johnson's Blue' is a hybrid with lavender-blue flowers above deeply cut leaves in early and mid-summer, making a plant about 30cm (1ft) high. A much larger species, growing to 1.2m (4ft), is *G. psilostemon*, with vivid black-centred magenta flowers and elegantly cut leaves. Others to look for are *G. macrorrhizum*, with aromatic leaves, and *G. wallichianum* 'Buxton's Variety', which has blue flowers with a distinctive white eye.

Geranium endressii 'Wargrave Pink'

Geum × borisii

Geum

(Avens) Rarely more than 30cm (1ft) high, *G. × borisii* is a useful plant for the front of a sunny or lightly shaded border, though its single orange-red flowers look particularly effective against a cooling green background. It thrives in ordinary soil, its rounded hairy leaves forming ground-covering rosettes. Almost twice as tall are strains of *G. chiloense*, which also flower over a long season in summer. 'Lady Stratheden' is yellow and 'Mrs Bradshaw' brick-red; both of these varieties have attractive double flowers.

Helleborus niger

(Christmas rose) The hellebores include some of the finest plants for the winter and early spring garden. The Christmas rose starts producing broad white flowers, sometimes tinged pink, from early winter, carried on 45cm (1½ft) stems above leathery dark green leaves. This hellebore does well in shade but will need regular top-dressing with rotted compost.

Helleborus orientalis

(Lenten rose) These hybrids produce wide cup-shaped flowers, ranging in colour from greenish white to·deep purple, and often beautifully speckled. Their season begins in late winter. Lenten roses grow to about 60cm (2ft), tolerate a wide range of soil conditions and do well in sun or shade. Their evergreen leaves make good ground cover.

Helleborus foetidus

(Stinking hellebore) Do not be put off by the name; *H. foetidus* is a garden plant of real quality, with handsomely divided ' evergreen leaves that can almost seem black. In sun or shade it will grow to 45cm (1½ft) tall and in winter produces pale green flowers with a maroon rim. Of comparable quality but a much larger plant is *H. corsicus*, which grows to a height of 90cm (3ft). It has good year-round foliage and in winter produces its highly distinctive green flowers.

Helleborus niger

Hemerocallis

(Day lily) Although individual flowers have only a fleeting life as their common name suggests, these lilies produce a succession of lovely blooms throughout summer and in the best forms these are carried elegantly on stems 90-150cm (3-5ft) tall above grassy foliage. Among the species, *H. flava* has exceptionally well-shaped yellow flowers and fine fragrance. The numerous hybrids include: 'Golden Chimes', rich yellow with reddish-brown reverse; 'Pink Damask', deep rose pink; and 'Stafford', dark red. All will grow in sun or light shade in ordinary soil that does not become to dry.

Heuchera

(Coral flower) A pretty ground-covering plant, *H. sanguinea* has dark, round evergreen leaves and hazy sprays of tiny red flowers throughout the summer. Excellent hybrids, most 45-60cm (1½-2ft) tall, include the deep coloured 'Bressingham Blaze'. They are all good for edging or underplanting and do well in light soils, in sun or part shade.

Hosta

(Plantain lily) Hostas are deservedly popular for they are outstanding foliage plants that also produce attractive lily-like flowers, predominantly in shades of violet and lilac but there are good whites too. Among the species there is a wide range from miniatures to substantial plants 90cm (3ft) or more in height. Breeders have taken advantage of this and variations in leaf shape, texture and colouring to produce a wide choice of hybrids.

H. fortunei 'Albopicta', growing to 45cm (18in), has large leaves marbled green and yellow, changing to two shades of green; *H. sieboldiana* 'Elegans', up to 75cm (2½ft) high,

Hosta fortunei 'Albopicta'

has deeply veined blue-grey leaves up to 30cm (1ft) across; 'Frances Williams' is similar but with a yellow margin to the leaf. 'Thomas Hogg' has a creamy edge to dark green leaves and flower stems to 60 cm (2ft) high. *H. undulata* 'Mediovariegata' makes a clump up to 45cm (1½ft) high with twisting leaves, cream at the centre with a dark green margin. Most hostas thrive in sun or shade in ordinary soil, perferably moisture retentive.

Iris

BEARDED HYBRIDS These are derived from *I. germanica*, and among the most sumptuous flowers of early summer, voluptuous in form, with erect standards and drooping falls, and sweetly scented. Furthermore, the texture of the flowers shows to advantage the wonderful subtlety and richness of their colour combinations. These irises are often grouped into three categories: dwarf, 45cm (1½ft) or less; intermediate, 45-75cm (1½-2½ft); and tall, 75-150cm (2½-5ft). Only the tall group needs staking but all require sun and good drainage in a soil that is neither too acid nor too rich. The rhizomes should be planted so that the tops are just showing.

IRIS SIBIRICA HYBRIDS These have smaller flowers than the bearded irises, grow to 90cm (3ft) and are suitable for planting in full sun by water or in borders where the soil is not too dry. The foliage is grassy and the predominantly blue or white flowers are borne in early and mid-summer. In the best of the new varieties the flowers are not too large and they are carried well clear of the leaves.

Kniphofia
(Red hot poker) The smaller kniphofia hybrids are invaluable plants for modern gardens, making manageable clumps of grassy leaves topped by stems 90cm (3ft) high carrying packed heads of tubular flowers. There are fiery shades, such as in 'Bressingham Flame', but also cooler colours, as in the creamy white of 'Maid of Orleans'. Flowering time – between early and late summer – depends on the variety. Kniphofias need full sun but do well in ordinary, well-drained soil.

Kniphofia 'Maid of Orleans'

Lupinus
(Lupin) The dense spikes of lupins are among the brightest accents of early summer, their brilliant candles rising to 1.2m (4ft) above soft green leaves divided into fingers. They are not happy in limy soil but otherwise are easy plants for sun or light shade, although generally not long lived. The Russell strain of hybrids offers a good colour range, including many multi-colours. Removal of the flower spikes as they fade will encourage the growth of secondary spikes.

Lychnis
(Campion) The purple-red flowers of L. coronaria are borne on a plant of branching grey and woolly foliage and stems that can grow to 90cm (3ft) tall. These boldly coloured flowers do well in dry sunny borders, where they self-seed freely.

Lupins (Russell Hybrids)

Meconopsis

(Himalayan blue poppy) Though not a plant for every garden – it does not like lime and does best in cool moist conditions – *M. betonicifolia* is so magnificent when well suited that it must be included in a selection of herbaceous perennials. In early and mid-summer stems up to 1.2m (4ft) high carry a succession of clear blue poppy flowers, sometimes nearly 10cm (4in) across, with golden stamens at the centre. A glade-like setting with light shade suits it well.

A relative of this splendid plant is the Welsh poppy, *M. cambrica*, a prodigious self-seeder but a welcome addition to the wild garden.

Monarda

(Bee balm, Oswego tea) In a sunny position with rich moist soil the aromatic bee balm, *M. didyma*, gives value through summer to early autumn. The clusters of tubular flowers, on stems up to 90cm (3ft) high, attract bees and butterflies. Two long-established and very reliable varieties to seek out are 'Cambridge Scarlet' and 'Croftway Pink'.

Meconopsis betonicifolia

Lychnis coronaria

Monarda didyma 'Cambridge Scarlet'

Nepeta × *faassenii* rarely exceeds a height of 45cm (1½ft)

Nepeta

(Catmint) The catmints are useful edging plants, producing sprays of lavender-blue flowers above aromatic grey-green foliage in early summer and later, if clipped over. Plant in full sun, in ordinary soil. 'Six Hills Giant' can grow to 75cm (2½ft) or more but the slightly less hardy *N.* × *faassenii* rarely exceeds a height of 45cm (1½ft).

Oenothera

(Evening primrose) Throughout the summer *O. missouriensis* – a species with flowers that last for several days – produces a long succession of large yellow blooms above stems that generally lie flat on the ground. Rarely more than 15cm (6in) high and thriving in sun, even in dry soils, this is an excellent plant for the front of a border.

Paeonia

PAEONY HYBRIDS These aristocrats, sometimes known as Chinese paeonies, have magnificent single or double flowers in a colour range that includes white, creams, pinks and reds. Plants form mounds of attractive foliage, often beautifully tinted, 90cm (3ft) or more high, and the flowering season falls between late spring and mid-summer.

Paeonies prefer well-drained but rich soil, in sun or light shade. A common cause for poor flowering is the crown being planted too deeply. A great favourite is 'Sarah Bernhardt', double, scented and with delicate pink flowers. However, almost all are delectable, so you can hardly go wrong.

PAEONY SPECIES No less appealing than the hybrids are numerous fine species, which require much the same growing conditions. In late spring the most sumptuous flower in many cottage gardens is the apothecaries' paeony, *P. officinalis*. The deep crimson fully double form 'Rubra-plena' makes a particularly impressive plant. Another beauty to look for is *P. mlokosewitschii*, with single pale yellow flowers. Both grow to about 60cm (2ft).

Papaver orientale

(Oriental poppy) These showy perennials for early summer have large flowers in a colour range that includes white, reds and pinks. The petals generally have dark blotches round the central knob. Plants do well in ordinary soil in full sun. Taller varieties may need staking and with all it is worth cutting back the foliage as it begins to die down to encourage a new crop of leaves.

Good medium to tall varieties, up to about 90cm (3ft), include: 'Goliath', blood-red; 'Perry's White', with a hint of pink; and 'Sultana', rose-pink. Shorter varieties include the scarlet 'Allegro' and the boldly blotched 'Black and White'.

Phlox

The varieties of *P. paniculata* come to their peak in late summer and are lovely planted in masses. There are pastel and deep tones in pink, red, purple and lavender, as well as white. The crowded flowerheads top stems about 90cm (3ft) high and the leggy base is best hidden behind elegant foliage such as that of geraniums. Grow in moisture-retentive soil in sun or light shade.

Polygonatum

(Solomon's seal) In early summer the slender arching stems of Solomon's seal, *P. × hybridum*, 60-120cm (2-4ft) tall, carry rows of tubular white flowers tipped with green. Once settled in a cool shady position – it is a natural woodlander for the wild garden – this easy perennial will slowly build up into manageable clumps, provided that you have planted them in soil that is moisture-retentive.

Paeonia officinalis 'Alba Plena', another impressively beautiful paeony

Pulmonaria saccharata 'Margery Fish'

Primula

(Primrose) There are many exotic or highly bred primroses but the simple beauty of the common primrose, *P. vulgaris,* is hard to match. The flowers are borne in great profusion in early and mid-spring, earlier if the weather is mild, forming mounds of soft yellow, about 30cm (1ft) high. They do well in sun or light shade, and like reasonably moist soil.

Pulmonaria

(Lungwort) In moist shady conditions *P. saccharata,* which has silver mottled leaves, makes attractive ground cover. In mid- and late spring the plants, about 30cm (1ft) high and sometimes twice this in spread, produce clusters of funnel-shaped flowers that open pink, turning blue as they age. 'Margery Fish' is a good variety that has particularly fine silvering of the leaves.

Pulsatilla vulgaris

(Pasque flower) Often grown in the rock garden, this is also a splendid plant for any sunny position with free-draining soil. In mid- to late spring silky buds open to mauve flowers with a bold centre of yellow stamens, and with ferny leaves, making a pretty plant about 30cm (1ft) high. The flowers are followed by fluffy seedheads. There are forms available that have more red or violet flowers.

Primula vulgaris (primrose)

Rheum palmatum

(Ornamental rhubarb) Not a plant for the small garden, this can make a base of handsomely jagged leaves up to 1.5m (5ft) across, with a flower spike in early summer up to 2.4m (8ft) tall. It is, however, a plant of noble proportions, growing most luxuriantly in moist conditions but doing reasonably well in ordinary soils. Full sun is needed to bring out the colour in forms such as 'Atrosanguineum' and 'Bowles' Variety', both of them suffused with red.

Spikes of *Salvia* × *superba* deepen from blue to purple

Veronica teucrium 'Crater Lake Blue'

Salvia

From mid-summer to autumn the blue changing to purple of *S.* × *superba* is most effective when plants form a group of three or more, the jagged dome, up to 90cm (3ft) high, making a splendid foreground to tall yellow flowers. Plant in free-draining soil, taking care to choose a position in full sun.

Sedum

A plant of long-lasting beauty at the end of summer, *S.* 'Autumn Joy' forms mounds of thick waxy foliage up to 60cm (2ft) high, topped by broad heads of pink flowers. These provide a late feast for bees and butterflies before gradually turning a deep bronzy red. Plant them in full sun in ordinary soil.

Veronica

(Speedwell) Most of the speedwells are easy plants for sunny positions with well-drained soil. The silver-grey leaves of *V. incana* form a year-round carpet from which rise spires of blue flowers throughout the summer, reaching a height of 30cm (1ft) or more. For flowers of intense gentian blue the best of the speedwells are some of the tall forms of *V. teucrium*, such as 'Crater Lake Blue', which grow to 45cm (1½ft).

INDEX AND ACKNOWLEDGEMENTS

Picture credits

John Glover: 16.
Harry Smith Horticultural Collection: 1, 4-5, 6, 7, 8(t,b), 9(t,b), 10, 13(tl,tr), 14(t,b), 15, 17(b), 18,
  21(t,b), 22, 23(t,b), 24, 25, 28(l,r), 30/1, 32(br), 33, 34(t), 35(bl,br), 37(b), 39(t).
Michael Warren: 17(t), 19, 26, 27, 29, 32(bl), 34(b), 36(t,b), 37(t), 38(l,r), 39(b), 40(t,b), 41, 42(t,b),
  43(t,bl,br), 44, 46(l,r), 47(t,b).

Artwork by Simon Roulstone.

48